Acting Out Yoga Presents:

ANNA IN PARIS

Written by:
Danielle Palli

Illustrated by:
Joan S. Peters

Birdland Media Works

"A huge thank you to Joan Peters for bringing Anna and Fondue's adventure to vivid life. And to my friends who helped with editing, marketing and research: Julie Chavanu, Cindy Readnower, Dusti Lewars and Lisa Ramirez, I am grateful. As always, I thank my husband, John Palli, for his endless love and support. Lastly, I'd like to thank Fondue. If he'd had been a well-behaved ferret, this book would not exist."
~Danielle Palli

"Many thanks to Danielle for giving me the opportunity to work on this fun project. What a perfect fit for a Parisian born illustrator. It also gave me an excuse to make a trip to Paris for some photographs and quick sketches of the various locations visited by Anna and Fondue. Thanks for introducing me to the world of ferrets and the "real" Fondue. Special thanks go to Amara Cocilovo-Nash for connecting me with Danielle, and to Frank Lynch for his loving support and suggestions. If you'd like to see more of my work, please visit www.joanpetersgallery.com."
~Joan Peters

Text copyright© 2013 Danielle Palli
Illustrations copyright© 2013 Joan S. Peters

All rights reserved. No part of the publication may be reproduced or transmitted in any form or by any means, electronic, mechanical, photocopying, recording or any information storage or retrieval system, without written permission from the publisher.

Requests for permission to make copies of any part of the work should write to:
Danielle@birdlandmediaworks.com

Published by Birdland Media Works 2013
www.birdlandmediaworks.com

Library of Congress Cataloging-in-publication Data
Palli, Danielle (author)
Peters, Joan (illustrator)

Acting Out Yoga Presents: Anna in Paris / Danielle Palli

ISBN: 978-0-5781242-7-8
Printed in the USA
First Edition
Printed and bound by 360Digital Books
Digital layout by Meredith Lamb
Edited by K. Lisa Ramirez

Yoga Poses

**Arch of Triumph
(Arc de Triomphe)**

Gargoyle

Eiffel Tower

Pyramid

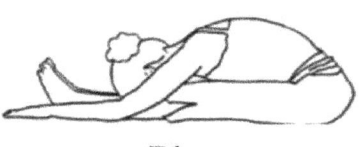

River

Dog

Snake

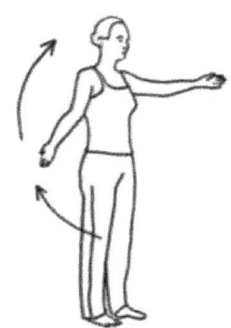

Clock

How the Acting Out Yoga Series Began

When I began teaching yoga some two decades years ago, instructing children of varied ages was a challenge. It wasn't always easy to find creative learning tools that would hold their attention and help them remember the poses (asanas).

I would ask, "Who can tell me something you learned today?" One child might remember a pose or two. When I would ask, "Who can show me…" and I would call out a pose, it was hit or miss recognition. One day, I announced, "Okay, time for silly story time!" I presented them with the cast of characters (i.e. a fire-breathing dragon or a mermaid) and began to tell them a made-up tale that they would act out using yoga poses. In some cases, I would assign characters just like a theater production saying, "Okay, you are the princess," or "You are the Archer." Not only would they take on that role, but occasionally I had them demonstrate the pose to the group for other students to follow.

At the end of class, I asked the question again, "Who can share with us something he or she learned today?" The hands went up enthusiastically, and wouldn't you know it? They remembered *every* pose.

I invite you to play. After all, playtime is Fondue's favorite pastime.
~Danielle Palli

How to Use This Book

Following the introduction, you will find that the pages on the LEFT side of the book serve as the instructor/parent guide, intended for elementary school teachers, parents and yoga instructors. On this page, you will find a brief "how to" for the poses and a photo, along with helpful information about the benefits and contraindications of a pose. You'll also be given tips for "acting out" the tale as well as modifications to advance or simplify a given pose based on a child's ability. On several of the pages, there are ideas for optional lesson plans to use during or after storytelling.

The pages on the RIGHT side of the book tell the fairy tale that can be read and appreciated simply as a children's story with colorful illustrations or as a creative learning tool.

When reading *Anna in Paris,* you will notice the poses are written in all capital, bold letters (i.e. **PYRAMID**) followed by an (R) or an (L) for asanas (poses) that require using the right or left side of the body, each in turn. Teachers, facilitators and parents should understand that the story is meant to be used in conjunction with an offering of warm-up exercises, as well as meditation and relaxation (if desired). However, if the children "act out" each of these poses in the order outlined within the story, they provide a balanced sequence.

Remember, that this is only a guide. On any one day, teachers/instructors/parents may choose to tell the tale of Anna and Fondue on the streets of Paris as a reading and comprehension tool. On another day, this book may be used as part of a yoga practice. On yet other days, Anna in Paris could be a resource for helping kids learn about the art and culture of France.

Disclaimer: The Acting Out Yoga books are meant to offer helpful information to parents, teachers and students of yoga. Practitioners should use proper discretion when using this book as an instructional guide, particularly when supervising young people who may be executing poses contained herein. Consult a health care professional before undertaking exercises described in this book. The author, illustrator and publisher expressly disclaim responsibility for any adverse effects that may result from the use or application of the information contained in this book.

Once upon a time in Paris, there lived a little girl named Anna. Anna had a mischievous pet ferret. She named him "Fondue" because Anna loved the cheese fondues her parents used to make on Saturday afternoons. Fondue liked to hide in small spaces where no one could see him—in handbags and under seat cushions—Anna once even discovered him sleeping in one of her father's slippers.

Fondue's favorite game was hide-and-seek, except that Fondue always did the hiding and Anna always did the seeking. He was also very fond of playing tag, usually giving Anna a light nip on her heel and then jumping back and forth like a heavyweight champion in a boxing ring. He'd let out a joyful, "heh, heh, heh," as Anna chased him around the room.

Like most ferrets, Fondue liked to burrow through things and would occasionally escape to the family greenhouse and dig up Mother's prize begonias. This did not make Anna's mother very happy.

However, Fondue had a habit like no other ferret. He liked to mimic the things he'd see around him by contorting his body into strange shapes. Anna was also convinced that he understood human conversation.

"No more playtime, Fondue." Anna plucked Fondue off of the top of her dresser. "I'm going to Paris for the day with *Maman*[1] and Papa, so you have to stay in your cage until we get back." She tucked her pet ferret into his hammock and closed the cage door.

1. *Maman* is the French word for "Mom."

Eiffel Tower
(Triangle)

How to:

1. Stand with your feet wide apart. Turn your right foot out so that it's perpendicular to your left foot.

2. Stretch your arms out parallel to the floor, no higher than your shoulders.

3. Reach toward your right toes and rest your hand on your leg. Stretch your left arm overhead and gaze toward your left hand.

4. Hold for three to five deep breaths before repeating on the other side.

Tip: Imagine that you'd like to roll your heart up to touch the sky as you bring your hips forward slightly. This should give you a deeper stretch across the chest and waist.

Modifications:

1. To advance the pose, touch your fingertips on the floor behind your leg as you stretch instead of resting your hand on your leg.

2. If you experience neck or eye strain while looking up, look toward the floor instead. To avoid shoulder soreness, keep your hand on your hip instead of extending it toward the sky.

Benefits:

- Stretches the hamstrings, calves, hips and chest.

- Strengthens the thighs.

- Sometimes referred to as the "happy pose" because of its ability to relieve stress.

Contraindications: Children suffering from headaches should avoid this pose. Those with shoulder or neck soreness should avoid this pose or use the #2 modification outlined above.

"Anna!" her mother called from another room. "Please, hurry or we'll miss the train!"

"I'll be right there!" Anna called back, and quickly pulled on her shoes and ran out of the room.

Fondue was just about to dose off when he heard a "click." Looking up, he realized that Anna had accidentally forgotten to latch the cage door shut. I'm going to Paris, he thought to himself, gleefully. Quickly slipping out of his cage, he scurried across the floor and into the main hallway where Anna and her parents were gathering their things.

"I hope you're in the mood for a picnic under the **EIFFEL TOWER (R)** today," Anna's father said, cheerfully.

Oh, goody!" Anna jumped up and down. "I love visiting the **EIFFEL TOWER (L)**!"

And, I love picnics, thought Fondue as he climbed into the basket without anyone noticing.

Calming Breath

Group Exercise: Anna is very nervous because she's worried her parents may discover that Fondue is hiding in the picnic basket. What do you do when you are worried or upset?

Instructions: Have each child sit in a chair or cross-legged on the floor. Ask them to place one palm on top of the other, face up, and rest their hands on their lap as if they were holding a small bowl.

Ask each child to take a deep inhalation, purse their lips (as if whistling) and let out an exhalation through their mouths. They should imagine they are exhaling their troubles into that imaginary bowl, relaxing as if they are sending their worries away.

After about a minute, have each child brush their palms together (as if they are dusting something off of their hands) allowing the imaginary worries to break apart and vanish into the floor.

They arrived at the station, and quickly boarded the train and settled in for their ride to Paris. Anna sat across from her parents with the picnic basket in the seat next to her. Curious to see if her mother had made her favorite cheese sandwiches, she snuck a peek into the basket.

"Aah!" Anna tried to muffle the sound as soon as she made it, letting out a cough so that no one would wonder what happened.

"Cover your mouth when you cough, dear," Anna's mother told her, and then returned to reading her book.

Anna nodded and peeked into the basket again. Inside, Fondue was nestled between a bottle of water and a plastic container that held the sandwiches. The paper towels that her mother had packed had been ripped to shreds in one of Fondue's burrowing frenzies.

Playtime? The little ferret looked up, inquiring. Anna shook her head "no" and closed the lid.

If her parents found out they would be very upset with her, but she knew she had to tell them. It was the right thing to do…but perhaps she would wait until they stopped for lunch, *after* she had a cheese sandwich.

Clock Pose
(Arm Circles)

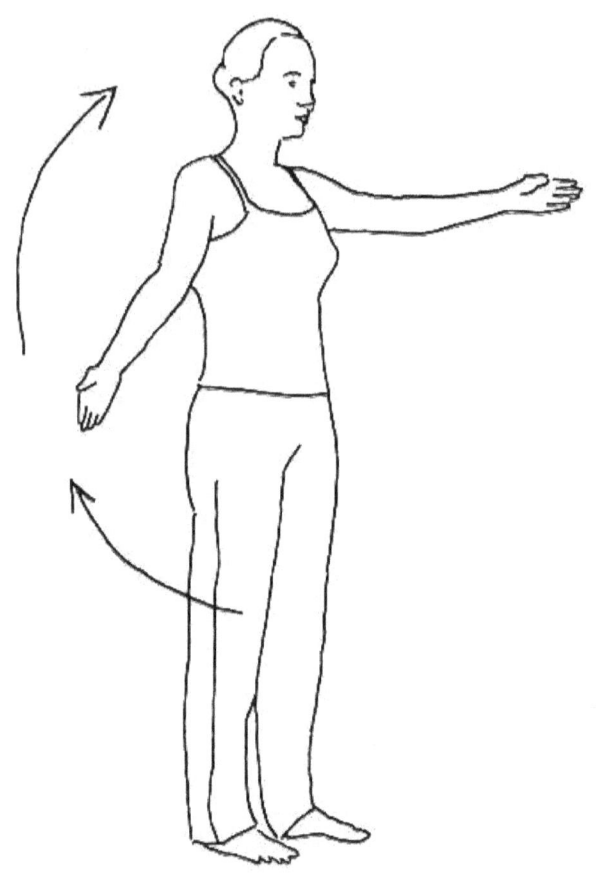

How to:

1. Stand comfortably and stretch your hands out in front of you with palms pressed together.

2. Slowly begin to raise your right arm overhead as if it were the arm of a clock reaching up toward 12 o'clock.

3. Continue the rotation behind you, turning your palm out as necessary and follow the circle around until your palms meet again in front of you.

4. Reverse the direction.

5. Repeat the sequence with your left arm.

Tip: See if you can begin to synchronize your breath with your movement, taking one complete inhalation and exhalation with each arm revolution.

Modifications:

If you have sore shoulders, you can modify this pose by stretching both arms out to the sides so that you're forming a "T" with your body. Slowly make small circles with your arms, forward and back, for several revolutions.

Benefits:

- Releases tension in the shoulders, preparing them for more exertion.
- Strengthens shoulder muscles.
- Helps maintain fluidity in the joints.

Those with shoulder injuries should consult a doctor before practicing **Clock** pose to avoid the potential for further injury.

Before long, Anna's family arrived at the Gare de Lyon station in Paris. It was bustling with people hurrying to and from their destinations.

"Anna," her father asked, "can you remember what year the Gare de Lyon was built?" Her father was a history teacher and always shared facts like this with his daughter.

"It was built for the World Exposition of 1900!" Anna declared, proudly.

"Very good, Anna!" Her father beamed.

Anna loved reading about the first World Exposition and wished she could have been there to see the colorful outdoor art exhibits, music concerts and theatrical displays. "We'd better get a move on," Anna's mother told them. "It's already 10 a.m." She motioned to the large **CLOCK** (R, L) tower at the entrance to the station.

Arch of Triumph
("Arc de Triomphe" or Bridge)

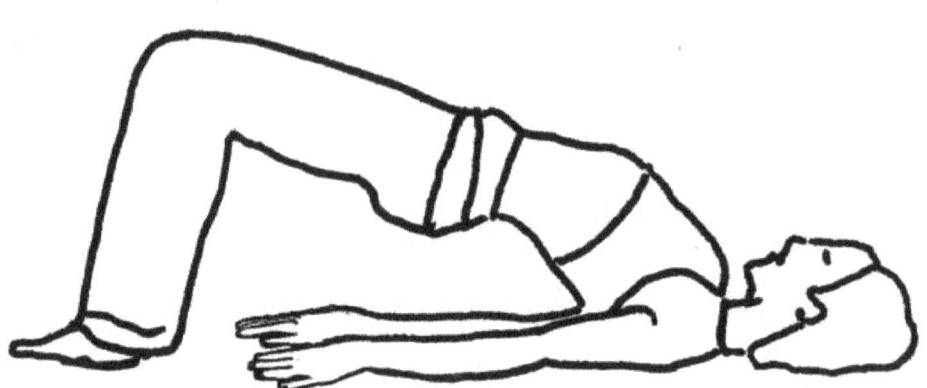

How to:

1. Laying on your back on your yoga mat, bend your knees and bring your feet flat to the floor with your knees approximately hips' distance apart.

2. Bringing your palms face down on the mat beside your hips, take a deep breath as you lift your hips high into the air and roll back so that your shoulders are supporting you.

3. Hold for three to five deep breaths. Then, relax your hips back to the mat.

Tip: If you are having trouble arching your back, try lining up your ankles under your knees and turn your feet out slightly.

Modifications:

To help release tension in the shoulders, try clasping your hands together under your body while your hips are lifted into the air.

Benefits:

- Strengthens the thighs, ankles, calves and low back.
- Creates flexibility in the spine.
- Helps energize the body.
- Stretches the chest and helps open the lungs.

Contraindications: Children with neck or low back injuries should avoid this pose.

Her father gathered up their belongings, including the picnic basket. "There's a taxi stand just over there." Her father pointed.

At the stand, they waited as a large woman with a poofy hat climbed into her taxi. "*À l'arc de triomphe, s'il vous plaît!*" she told the driver. ("To the **ARCH** of Triumph, if you please.") Just as the taxi pulled away from the curb, Anna noticed something peculiar protruding from the woman's hat. It looked almost like a tail.

Are Ferrets Really That Mischievous?

Fondue is a curious ferret. Do all ferrets like to explore? As an exercise, make a list of activities Fondue enjoys, such as:

- Likes to dig up mother's flowers.
- Hides in father's shoes.
- Likes to play games.

Ask or assist each child to research ferrets and share what they've learned. It could be about behavior, where they come from, what they eat, or how to take care of them.

Here are a few helpful facts to get you started:

- Ferrets are pure meat-eaters—no veggies for them!
- Even healthy ferrets sleep a minimum of 15 hours a day.
- Their eyesight may be weak, but their sense of smell and hearing make up for it!
- Ferrets love to play and often make chirping noises as they jump to and fro and run around the room.
- Ferrets are very affectionate and love when their caretakers "groom" them by gently "plucking" at their fur. (Note: Just pull very lightly. Don't hurt your ferret by pulling out fur!)
- Ferrets are natural-born burrowers and love having bedding or a box filled with shredded paper through which to dig.
- Ferrets get their teeth brushed and nails clipped—just like people!

"Aah!" Anna squealed and looked in horror at the picnic basket. Its lid was now open and Fondue was nowhere inside. Impulsively, Anna did the only thing she could think of. She began running after the taxi, darting in between crowds of people yelling, "Fondue, wait for me!" Her parents tried to follow her, but a little girl in a big crowd was as difficult to catch as a ferret loose on the streets of Paris.

Meanwhile, Fondue curled up under the woman's hat and—as ferrets often do—fell fast asleep. He didn't awaken until the woman had reached her destination, the **ARCH** of Triumph. When he did, the woman stepped out of the cab, and the weight of a certain ferret sent her hat toppling to the ground. As the driver went to fetch it for her, Fondue made his escape.

Let's Review!

What have we learned so far?

- Eiffel Tower Pose (also called "Triangle Pose").
- Clock Pose.
- Arch of Triumph Pose, or simply, Arch Pose (also called "Bridge Pose").

Ask for three volunteers to demonstrate each of the poses they've learned so far; one can play the "instructor" and offer verbal cues to the other two "students." The entire group can review these poses together.

Note: Make sure that for Eiffel Tower and Clock poses, the group practices each of them on the right and left sides.

Being a curious creature, Fondue was determined to follow a group of tourists to the very top of the historic site. After all, it was the largest of its kind in the world, completed in 1836. This, Fondue learned when Anna's father was talking one night over dinner and thought Fondue couldn't understand him.

When he reached the top of the monument, he looked out over the entire city. *There is so much to see,* thought Fondue. Where shall I begin? As if in answer, a young tourist walked by and said to her friend, "You just can't come to Paris without walking down Champs-Elysées. It's one of the most famous streets in the world and you won't find boutiques and cafés anywhere like the ones you'll find there." Fondue wasn't sure what a boutique was, but he did know the word "café" and that meant *food*! He scurried down the steps of the monument and followed the tourists on their path to Champs-Elysées.

Dog
(Downward Facing Dog)

How to:

1. Begin with your hands and knees on your mat so that your wrists are lined up under your shoulders and your knees are in line with your hips. Keep your toes pulled back so that you are resting on the balls of your feet.

2. Inhale. Then, as you exhale, lift your knees off the mat (straightening your legs) and roll back as if trying to touch your hips to the sky, forming an upside-down "V."

3. Spread your fingers wide as you continue to press into the mat. Your heels may or may not touch the mat.

Instructor/Parent Tip: If you notice children with tension in their shoulders (i.e. they look more like they are in a push up position than an upside-down "V"), ask them to bend their knees slightly and roll back and up (as if touching their tailbone to the sky). They can then straighten their legs, if they are comfortable doing so.

Modifications:

1. Advance the pose by raising one leg up off the ground behind you, as high as you can, while holding your Dog Pose.

2. Simplify this pose by bending your knees slightly as you push your hips up toward the sky.

Benefits:

- Stretches the hamstrings and calves.
- Opens and strengthens the shoulders, arms and legs.
- Relieves back tension and overall fatigue.

Contraindications: Children with an upset stomach should avoid this pose. Children with wrist injuries should avoid this pose.

When he reached the famous street, Fondue was drawn in by the smells of baked baguettes wafting from one of the local bakeries. He pressed his face against the window, his eyes wide with fascination at the rows and rows of fresh bread that he could so easily dig through.

"A rat!" someone screamed, jarring Fondue from his dreamlike state. He looked around, frantically, but the only "rat" he saw was his own reflection in the window.

I'm not a rat! He thought, indignantly. *As a matter of fact, I happen to be from weasel, badger and sea otter lineages.*

He quickly forgot about being angry when he noticed that the shopper dropped a bag containing a ham and cheese croissant sandwich as he darted away. Fondue snatched the sandwich quickly and scooted off before anyone else could claim it.

Fondue found a cool spot in the shade under a horse-chestnut tree, where he nibbled on a bit of ham and watched as a local artist on the street sketched the scenery. Among the people who passed by was a young man walking his **DOG.** The leash reminded him of the one Anna used to take him out when they went for walks. Suddenly, he missed his caretaker. *Where did she say she was going? Aha!* He remembered.

Create a Collage!

What you'll need:

- Pictures of Paris (or France, in general).
- Large Poster Board.
- Drawing Paper.
- A Stick of Glue.
- Crayons.
- Plastic Scissors.

Find magazine or printed Internet photos, pictures or words on a page that represent Paris or France. You'll also need one poster board and a stick of glue.

Distribute the photos among the children and invite them to take turns gluing their photo onto the poster board, anywhere they choose. There should be large white gaps left on the board.

Next, ask each child to draw a picture of Fondue, Anna or any Parisian location they learned about in the story. Help them cut out the drawings and add them to the collage.

Afterward, point out different images and have the group explain what they are seeing. Hang the masterpiece up for the group to enjoy.

After Anna lost sight of Fondue, she realized that she also misplaced her parents. Fortunately, she was a clever little girl, and knew how to take the metro to the station where they originally planned to go, the **EIFFEL TOWER** (R). Built by Gustave Eiffel in 1889, the **EIFFEL TOWER** (L) has become the symbol of France. The names of famous French scientists and engineers of that time period are engraved on it, honoring their contributions to the scientific world.

When Anna arrived at the monument, Fondue spotted her immediately. Ferrets can only see the colors red, blue, black and white. Fortunately, Anna had bright red hair and was easy to pick out from the crowd.

Playtime!

While in **DOG** pose, have a little fun. Let kids wag their pretend tails, shout out their best bark or walk on all fours.

You can even play "Anna says," a variation of "Simon says." Just make sure to include lots of breaks where kids can rest their knees on the floor and give their tired arms a break.

Anna says, "Wag your tail!"

Anna says, "Let out a dog howl!"

"Lift one paw off the ground!" *Uh oh? Anna didn't say that!*

Anna says, "Lift one paw off the ground."

Note: No child is ever "out," even if Anna *didn't say*. Everyone gets a "good job!" for playing.

"Fondue!" Anna scooped up her furry friend when he nipped at her heel. "I was so worried about you!" She hugged him and scratched the back of his head affectionately. Just then, a little **DOG** ran by.

Playtime! thought Fondue, and he leapt from her arms and began running after his new playmate with Anna following closely behind.

River
(Seated Forward Bend)

How to:

1. Sit on the floor with your legs straight in front of you, feet several inches apart.

2. Flex your feet as you inhale and reach your arms overhead (as if to touch your fingertips to the sky). Palms are turned inward.

3. Exhale and reach toward your toes, resting your hands anywhere that you can reach comfortably (toes, shins, etc.).

4. Take three to five deep breaths, then slowly roll up to sitting.

Tip: You'll get a deeper stretch by sitting tall and keeping your back straight as you bend forward.

Modifications:

1. Advance this pose by holding the outside of your feet in your forward bend. You may even be able to rest your stomach on the tops of your thighs.

2. Simplify by bending your knees slightly and holding on to your shin or ankles.

Benefits:

- Stretches the hamstrings, spine and shoulders.
- Improves digestion.
- Promotes relaxation.

Contraindications: Children with an upset stomach should avoid this pose. Children with asthma should only practice this pose if approved by their family physician.

Fondue didn't stop running until he'd reached the Batobus, a boat taxi that travels the Seine **RIVER**. It stops at various historic sites in Paris for the many visitors that wish to see them. He scurried on board and squirmed his way under one of the seats. Anna, being little herself, managed to slip past the boat attendants unnoticed. She found her pet in the back of the Batobus and took a seat.

The boat's next stop was the Musée d'Orsay (the Orsay Museum). Originally a train station, the building was converted into a museum in 1986. It houses the works of famous artists such as Monet, Renoir, Degas and other French Impressionists.

"Just a reminder," the captain said over the loudspeaker, "The Orsay Museum is free on the first Sunday of the month, making today the perfect day to visit!"

Snake
(Cobra Pose)

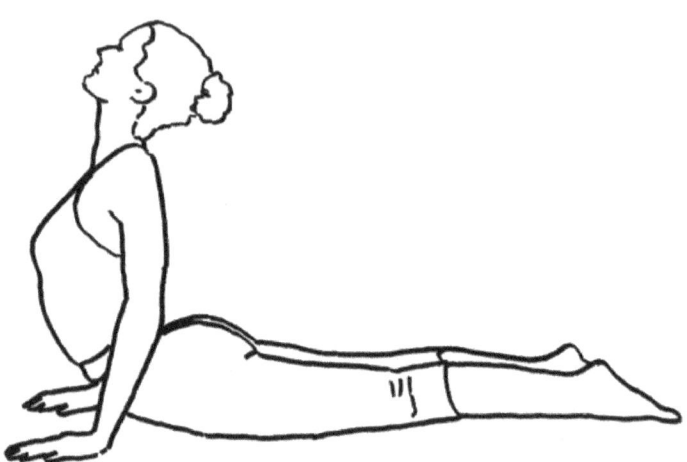

How to:

1. Lay on your stomach with your legs stretched out, feet several inches apart and the tops of your toes touching the floor.
2. Place your palms under your shoulders and inhale as you press into your hands and straighten your arms slowly, arching your back.
3. Tuck your chin slightly as your eyes gaze up toward your forehead.
4. Take three to five deep breaths and lower back down.

Tip: Keep the hips touching the floor and press your shoulders down, away from your ears, allowing you to lengthen your spine fully.

Modifications:

1. Advance this pose by bending the knees and seeing if you can touch your toes to the top of your head.
2. Simplify this pose by coming up onto your forearms and keeping your elbows bent as you lightly arch your back.

Benefits:

- Strengthens the spine.
- Stretches the chest, shoulders and abdomen.
- Promotes deeper breathing by stretching the lungs.
-

Contraindications: Children with low back injuries should avoid this pose. Children with sensitive low backs should practice modification #2.

Fondue's ears perked up. *Free!* That was the perfect price for a ferret with no money. He darted off the Batobus with Anna following closely behind. Once inside the museum, Fondue didn't stop running until he reached a painting that caught his attention. It was the *Serpent Charmer* by Henri "Douanier" Rousseau.[1] Even though the painting looked gray to him, he recognized the **SNAKE** that was coiled around the woman's neck in the picture. He saw a similar one in the greenhouse once, but that one was much smaller.

1. Henri Rousseau is nicknamed "Douanier Rousseau" because he was a customs officer in addition to being an artist. "Douanier" is the French word for "customs officer."

Learn about Art

Gather several books or Internet articles featuring the museums of Paris and show the children samples of paintings by Claude Monet, Pierre-Auguste Renoir and Leonardo Da Vinci. Ask the children which paintings they like best and why.

Alternatively, have one or two children look up Monet's *Blue Water Lilies* or Rousseau's *Serpent Charmer* on a computer. Talk briefly about Impressionism and ask the group what they notice about the paintings.

- Are they dark or light?
- What colors and textures stand out?
- How does the picture make you feel?
- What's happening in the painting?

"That's a pretty picture," Anna told Fondue. "But I like Monet's water lilies better. You'll like it too, Fondue. It's mostly blue! C'mon, I'll show you." After they visited the painting *Blue Water Lilies*, by Claude Monet, they headed back to the Batobus and continued their boat trip down the **RIVER**.

Gargoyle
(Inner Thigh Stretch)

How to:

1. Kneel on the floor and sit back on your heels (on the tops of your feet). Open your knees outward as wide as is comfortable.
2. Bend forward and rest your elbows on the floor, head in your hands.
3. Keep pressing your "sit" bones back toward your heels for a deeper inner thigh stretch.
4. Hold for three to five deep breaths.

Tip: If your feet begin to cramp, stretch the toes back so that you are resting on the balls of your feet and not the tops of your toes. Stretch your arms out in front (palms down) for an additional stretch across the chest and shoulders.

Modifications:

1. Advance the pose by separating the feet hips' distance apart and turning them outward. Now you will be resting on the sides of your feet with your big toes on the floor and pinky toes facing the ceiling.
2. If this is too strenuous on the knees, place a pillow or bolster under your hips or only sit back halfway.

Benefits:

- Stretches the inner thighs, knees and hips.
- Stretches the low back.
- Tones the upper back and stretches the chest (when straightening the arms out in front).

Contraindications: Children with knee or ankle injuries should avoid this pose.

Anna knew that her parents were probably getting worried, but she couldn't help but think how much Fondue would like to see the Notre-Dame Cathedral. "Okay, Fondue," Anna said, looking down at him. "One more stop before home. I bet you've never seen a **GARGOYLE** before!" Fondue hopped happily from side to side and let out a cluck. He didn't know what they were, but he was certain he would like them.

Once they reached the large church, Anna pointed upward. Throughout the upper exterior of Notre-Dame sat these large monsters carved out of stone. They were once believed to frighten away evil spirits. Fondue could understand that. They were much scarier than the **SNAKE** he saw earlier.

What Should You Do if You Are Lost?

In this story, Anna didn't know where her parents were. What would you do if you were Anna or Fondue in a big city and trying to find your parents?

1. Stay in one place. Your parents will already be looking for you.

2. Wherever you are, see if there is a police officer near you. If not, do you see a mother with her child? Someone working nearby? If so, tell them your first and last name and that you are lost. Also, tell them your parents' names.

Note: Do not get into the car of a stranger nor enter the house of someone your parents have not given you permission to visit.

Who could Anna have found to help her in this story?

- A police officer.
- A security guard working at the museum.
- An attendant working on the Batobus.

They were just about to go inside the cathedral when Anna felt a hand on her shoulder. Looking up, she saw a police officer smiling down at her. "Is your name Anna, by chance?" she asked. Anna nodded, snatching Fondue by the scruff of his neck and cradling him across her arm.

"Your parents are very worried and have been trying to find you all day. Let's get you back to your family." The officer made a call to Anna's father and handed her the phone. He told her that it was okay to go with the police officer, so Anna followed the officer back to her police car. As soon as Anna settled in the passenger side, Fondue fell fast asleep in her arms.

"Are we going to the police station?" Anna inquired. "No," the officer replied. "We spotted another little red-headed girl that looked like you at the Louvre museum. Since your parents are already there, we'll just go and meet them."

Pyramid

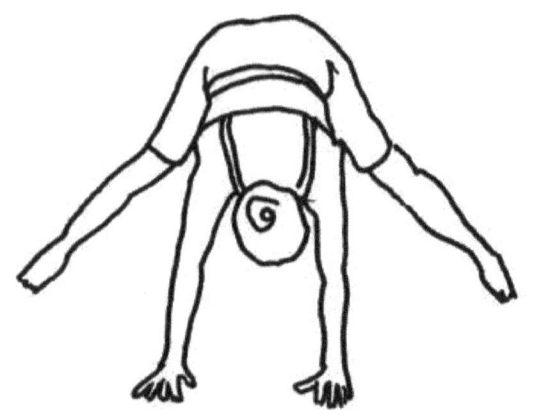

How to:

1. Stand in a wide straddle with your feet flat on the floor.
2. Place your hands on your hips and inhale. As you exhale, bend forward with a flat back.
3. Stretch your arms out in front, palms down on the floor. Your arms should be straight and your back flat.
4. Hold for three to five deep breaths, pressing the hips back and up slightly for a deeper stretch.
5. To come out of this pose, walk your hands back so that your weight is centered over your hips. Bring your hands to your waist and inhale as you straighten to standing.

Tip: To add on to this stretch, try "walking" your hands over to your right leg for several deep breaths, then to the left. Return to the center for two more breaths.

Modifications:

1. Advance this pose by separating your feet slightly while in this stretch. Bend your arms and see if you can comfortably touch the top of your head to the floor.
2. Simplify this pose by reaching down to touch the fingertips to the floor only (instead of stretching the arms out in front).

Benefits:

- Stretches the inner thighs, hamstrings and hips.
- Tones the abdominal muscles and shoulders.
- Stretches the low back.

Contraindications: Children with sensitive lower backs should use modification #2.

Anna's parents waited anxiously at the **PYRAMID**, the Louvre's main entrance. When they saw her holding Fondue, they each wrapped their arms around her, giving her a big hug. They thanked the police officer before the officer got back into her car and drove away.

"Anna," her mother scolded, "please don't ever scare us like that again!"

"I'm sorry, *Maman*," Anna told her, "but Fondue had never seen a **GARGOYLE** before!" Her mother looked confused, so Anna told her about their day.

"Sounds like quite an adventure," her father remarked.

"Oh, it was!" Anna was excited. "Wait, before we go home, can we please take Fondue into the Louvre? He loves museums, and he's never seen the painting of Mona Lisa or the statue of Venus de Milo."

Let's Review!

What poses did you learn today?

Invite kids to call out poses and briefly ask them to demonstrate each one. Did they get them all?

Arch of Triumph (Arc de Triomphe)

Gargoyle

Eiffel Tower

Pyramid

River

Dog

Snake

Clock

"Not today," her mother laughed, looking down at Fondue, who couldn't stop yawning from being so tired. "It looks like Fondue's journey concludes at the **PYRAMID**."

They decided to take the Paris Metro back to the Gare de Lyon station. Anna looked up at the large **CLOCK** (R, L) tower. It was exactly 6 p.m.

www.ingramcontent.com/pod-product-compliance
Lightning Source LLC
Chambersburg PA
CBHW061750290426
44108CB00028B/2947